THE MID TYNE VILLAGE﹚ NORTHUMBERLAND

A history in photographs of Ovingham, Ovington, Stocksfield, Mickley, Eltringham and Low Prudhoe

Selected and annotated by Douglas Mennear

Northumberland
Library
A County Council Service

First published in 1993 by Northumberland County Library,
The Willows, Morpeth, Northumberland NE61 1TA

Copyright © Douglas Mennear and Northumberland County Library 1993

Printed by Pattinson and Sons, Newcastle upon Tyne

British Library Cataloguing-in-Publication data

A catalogue record for this book is available from the British Library

ISBN 1 874020 09 4

FRONT COVER

OVINGHAM from the Prudhoe Bank c.1885 - the Toll Bridge had been open about a year - 20 December 1883. The vicarage and stables are clearly shown, the Reading Rooms on the west side of the bridge had not yet been built. The vicarage is now largely hidden by trees. The high water mark of the great 1771 flood is half way up the third terrace wall of the vicarage. The Ovingham river bank has moved 50 yards towards Prudhoe in the last 110 years - 20 yards in the last 30 years.

(Reproduced with the permission of the Gibson Collection)

INTRODUCTION

This volume covers a number of mid Tyne Villages connected by, or more correctly divided by, a common factor - the River Tyne. Ovingham is the oldest village, located where it is because of a ford (at one time there were three fords). The existing church is just over 1,000 years old, but the village was established in about the 7th century. Ovington is the daughter settlement one and a half miles up the hillside, and until the 1960s was, surprisingly, always larger than Ovingham.

Stocksfield/Painshawfield, Mickley, Eltringham Colliery and Low Prudhoe are south of the river. Fords and ferries were always important - with five ferries and eight fords between Bywell and Wylam, but floods greatly affected life, preventing people getting to and from work, church and school. The most used fords were at Bywell and Ovingham. Bywell, after decades of being without a bridge, was provided with one in 1836 by the owner of Bywell. Thomas Bewick campaigned for a bridge at Ovingham, but it was only in December 1883 that the Ovingham Bridge Company provided the toll bridge which is still in use today. The Eltringham Ferry at Mickley Junction lasted until 1962/3.

Bywell, three miles upstream from Ovingham, was a small town in the mid 16th century with two churches, 15 shops, inns, a market, blacksmiths etc but the village houses and businesses were all removed by the mid 19th century. Some of the villagers were rehoused in the Stocksfield area - out of sight of the Hall.

Stocksfield Painshawfield Estate has had an unusual history - originally being an area of scattered farms. The Newcastle - Carlisle Railway, a very early railway, had a major effect on the Tyne valley, and Newcastle businessmen escaped from industrialised Tyneside to live near the then new railway stations from the 1860s. In 1895 a group of Trustees set up the Newcastle Allotments Association and bought three farms - Batt House, Birches Nook and Painshawfield - initially to split into plots of nine acres, but over the years smaller but still large plots were offered for individual detached houses. Controlled in-filling by the 99 year old Estate Committee and, since 1947, also by the planning authorities, has continued since the Estate was set up in the last century, and planting of trees in the gardens has turned farmland into domestic woodland.

Mickley, Eltringham and Low Prudhoe grew as a result of the development of a large number of small collieries, coal drifts, brickworks, cokeworks and pipeworks - and then declined, almost to the state of extinction, though the site at Mickley Square was redeveloped in the early 1960s and its character has been totally changed. Mickley Junction was a railway hamlet, but all that now remains is a single house.

Research into these photographs has revealed the extent of local small industries - water mills at Ridley Mill and Whittle Mill; many collieries or drifts on the south side of the river at Low Prudhoe, Eltringham, Mickley and as far west as Painshawfield Estate; and a pipeworks, brickworks, cokeworks, milk depot/creamery, bleachworks, dyeworks and three breweries.

The sidings on the quay between Mickley Junction and Low Prudhoe have gone. The sidings immediately west of Prudhoe Station, and its goods facilities have been removed and the same has occurred at Stocksfield. Both the rope-hauled rail line for single wagons to Eltringham Colliery and the narrow gauge line for rakes of small trucks carrying clay and coal between West Mickley and Eltringham have gone. But evidence of such former industrial activities remains in some places.

Other changes have made major alterations to the faces of the villages presented in this booklet, particularly the planting and retention of trees, most noticeable at Ovingham and on the Painshawfield Estate. All villages have had gradual character changes as a result of individual building "improvements", with the alteration in size and shape of windows, addition of porches, use of PVC window frames, formation of picture windows, and replacement of old doors with "sunburst" feature doors. So many of the buildings in the villages are older than they look because of recently fashionable modernisation. Visually, Ovington has probably changed least of all, and "The beautification" of its rough, open spaces in the 1920s now results in it frequently winning the Northumberland Small Villages, Best Kept Village Competition. This "Beautification" was devised by the then Vicar of Ovingham, but was originally resisted by the Ovingham villagers.

Armed with this Local History Booklet, you will be able to step back as much as 125 years, by putting yourself on the spot where the original photographer was when he took his photograph. Prepare to be surprised!

ACKNOWLEDGEMENTS

Thank you to all those listed below for providing historical information and/or photographs, but particularly to Mr Ron Edgar of Ovingham, who for many years has been the unofficial historian of Ovingham. If I have inadvertantly omitted anyone then please accept my apologies.

Mr D Archer, Mr R Edgar *, Miss C Elliot, Mr F Hetherington, Mr H Outterside, Mrs M Robson, Miss J Stokoe *, Mrs D Turner, Mrs M Watson, AirFotos, The Gibson Collection, Mr W Forster, Mrs C Graham, Mr K Jarvis, Mrs P Maddison, Mrs M Oram, Mrs W Oram *, Mr & Mrs W Weatherspoon, Mr R M Browell, Mr & Mrs Donnelly, Mr R Rourke, Mrs M Thompson *, Mrs D Baxter *, Mrs J Glaister, Mr A Harrison, Mr A Johnson, Mr I Seymour *, Mrs E Johnson *, Mrs S McGlen, Mr G Brown, Mr & Mrs R Ackroyd, Mr L Carr, Mr P R B Brookes, Mr K L Taylor *, Dr C Warn *, Dr W Fawcett, Author's collection *, Busways Travel Services Ltd * Northumberland County Record Office * and Prudhoe Library.*

Permission to use postcards and photographs are shown *

Douglas Mennear

POPULATION CHANGES 1801 - 1991

	1801	1861	1871	1881	1891	1901	1911	1921	1931	1951	1961	1971	1981	1991
Ovingham	253	277	226	280	328	487	399	526H	393	460	556	935	1147	1238
Ovington	344	420	446	533	508	471	504	660H	470	628H	411	355	519	541
Stocksfield	260	478	473	389	676	941	1493	1853	1741	1837	2035	2285	2281	3034#
Mickley	186	566	1203	1371	1450	1709	2264*	2365*	2134*	1862*	1432*	1570*	1794*	1054#
Eltringham	24	159	144	451	522	563	466	456	439	324	320	40	40	40
Low Prudhoe	62	490	588	844	929	846	748	645	500	300	180	130	130	130
Totals in the villages	**1129**	**2390**	**2930**	**3868**	**4303**	**5017**	**5874**	**6505**	**5677**	**5411**	**4834**	**5315**	**5911**	**6037**
Prudhoe	318	471	1995	3041	3391	3901~	4734	4734	5626	8265	7166	7129	9190	8980~

This table shows the population growth (and decline) of the various villages from 1801. In the case of Mickley, Eltrigham and Low Prudhoe approximations have been made.

~ For comparison, Prudhoe household population excludes the population of Prudhoe Hall. Prudhoe became an Urban District in 1901. In the above table, populations for Prudhoe exclude Low Prudhoe, Mickley and Eltringham which since 1901 have been administratively within the UD boundary.

* From 1911 there was an enclave of Mickley Ward into Stocksfield Parish. # After 1981 the boundaries of Mickley Ward and Stocksfield Parish were amended to include Birkdene and the east side of New Ridley Road in Stocksfield. 700 population were transferred from Mickley Ward to Stocksfield Parish.

H In 1951 the Ovington Parish figure included considerable holiday population, in holiday bungalows and under canvas. 1921 figures for both Ovington and Ovingham included holiday population.

Ovingham Toll Bridge Opening Ceremony - 20 December 1883. The lack of a bridge, and dependence on ford and ferry when the river was not high, was keenly felt. Thomas Bewick wrote in 1816 to the Newcastle Courant under the nom de plume of "The Hermit of Ovingham", pressing for a bridge, and there was pressure for almost another 70 years. The Ovingham Bridge Toll Company built the cast iron bridge which was freed from toll on 5 July 1945. In 1993 this same bridge is still most important and much used but there is now an adjacent separate footbridge.

Ovingham Bridge and Reading Room in 1936, showing the narrow, all purpose bridge to Prudhoe until 1974, when a separate footbridge was constructed on the downstream side. The 1883 bridge was, and still is restricted to bicycles, horses and now also small cars and vans. The toll house can be seen on the other side of the river and the rows of houses of Low Prudhoe. The Reading Room dates from 1894 and has retained its name, but is now also known as the Village Hall. Until World War II it was used by subscribers only, primarily by the men of the village to read newspapers, play billiards etc, and to a lesser extent by the women for special events such as concerts and sales of work. The highly decorated building was to celebrate the 25th Anniversary of King George V.

Ovingham West End - c.1880. Looking east from the ford at the Whittle Burn to the Church. A cottage and implement shed occupy the site of what is now the Post Office, flat and house. Nos 1, 2 and 3 West End Row had not been built. On the right is a cottage/stables and store room which went with The Bridge End Inn beyond. The White Cottage with its stone flagged roof (and trained fruit tree) remain albeit as an almost detached room of a modern house.

Ovingham, west end 1880, looking towards Ovington and the ford. The Churchyard wall and Glebe Farm farmhouse are on the right. Grey Cottage is behind the tree on the left backing up against Front Row (River View) Cottages. The cottage with shutters and implement shed, with its doors used as a village notice board, is where the Post Office is now. The Church School and schoolhouse are in the background.

Ovingham, the north side of the Church c.1910. The cottage is where the garden known as Jimmy Johnson's garden is located. The two flats beyond occupy what has become the small village car park. The cottage was condemned in 1904 and offered to the Church for £90 but this was not taken up. The flats were owned by an absentee landlord, and were finally demolished in 1956. They had gas and water inside, but the drain was outside. They shared a two-hole ash toilet. During World War II they were used for billeting sergeants after the retreat from Dunkirk. The Reading Room was used for billeting soldiers, and Greenhaugh House for Officers.

Ovingham west end c.1910 showing the ford (bridged in 1936) and the Packhorse Bridge, where the Proclamation of the Goose Fair is now made in June each year. Even with the (rather low) road bridge the River Tyne and Whittle Burn can still flood, to the extent of preventing traffic between the village and Ovington & Bywell, and also preventing pedestrians from using the Packhorse Bridge. Children at Ovingham's new First and Middle Schools are still occasionally sent home until the floods subside. The building in the foreground has had a variety of uses stables, store and toilet for the pub; cottage, bakery, shop, assembly room; and in 1993 bedrooms for the Bridge End Inn.

Ovingham c.1925. The Bridge End Inn is next to the Packhorse Bridge. This is one of the three oldest buildings in Ovingham, though the date of building is not known, nor the precise date of this photograph. The locations of The Salmon, The Black Bull, The White Horse and The Hare and Hounds are not known. The latter may have been the Hare and Hounds within 250 yards of Cherryburn at Mickley which was demolished in 1962/3. The tailpiece wood engraving in Bewick's *British Birds Vol* I of 1805 known as "The Ovingham Dyers" - shows this pub before extension and alterations. Bewick in his Memoir stated there were four inns with signs which he copied in his youth at Ovingham but there are no records of them.

Ovingham, The White Swan (Hotel), formerly the Ovingham Inn - pre 1928. This beautifully simple late Georgian country building had an unfortunate exterior ground floor restyling in the late 1950s early 1960s, which was improved in 1990, by simplification including the removal of pseudo shutters. There is a planning permission to further restore it to its original condition. The brewery behind the pub, Ovingham House adjacent (the original farmhouse for Brewery Farm), and what is now known as Brewery Farm (previously known as Brick House) all belonged to the Bedlington Family until 1928. Then the estate was acquired by Sydney Bates, owner of the Mickley Coal Company - hence the National Coal Board ownership of Brewery Farm, until recently. The foundations of the brewery are beneath the beer garden at the rear. A cart is shown emerging from the brewery which ceased brewing about 1928. Note the mounting block close to the near corner of the pub. Other pubs supplied from Ovingham Brewery included the Black Bull at Wylam and one at Mickley - perhaps the former Miners Arms.

A posed photograph of Ovingham School, with the school master's house - before 1896 (the house windows are to the left and right of the door). It is thought the building was constructed in 1815 - contributed to by the people of the village, and thereafter part-maintained by the Diocesan Board. It was used until 1963 when the new First School was opened. The Whittle Burn at times floods the school and School House, the last time being April 1992. The burn has always been a fascination and pupils found it was useful to fall into when they did not like a forthcoming lesson and wished to be sent home.

Ovingham c.1870 from the north west across the Whittle Burn. This shows the rear of the School which was very small at that time, before the Post Office was built and before the White Cottage became White the two storey outbuildings in front of the Bridge End Inn are in their original condition. Prudhoe Castle can be seen on the skyline. This view is impossible to obtain today as there are 100 ft trees obscuring it along the burn side. This photograph had been lost to the village from about 1873 - and was turned up by chance from a relative of the family which took it - who by then had no idea of where the photograph had been taken.

Whittle Mill Farm from the south c.1900. The overshot metal wheel was in the lowest of the range of buildings. The Mill was situated in Whittle Dene half a mile north of Ovingham by direct footpath but accessible by horse and cart only from Ovingham and Whittle Farm. The Mill (and Dye Works and Bleach Works) were affected by the lack of constant water as a result of the construction of the first Whittle Dene Reservoir in 1848 which drew from more than half of the area drained by the Whittle Burn. The last bleaching was about 1865. The Mill struggled on until well into this century at times when there was sufficient water.

WHITTLE MILL, OVINGHAM 3942. G.H. N/c

Whittle Mill looking downstream, possibly 1910. It was not the burn which fed water directly to the mill, but the iron pipe, shown on the photo, leading out of the mill ponds. The mill pond(s) were fed by a 750 yard system of tunnels and open channels from a weir, - all of which can still be traced in 1993. Even the construction of a second mill pond could not provide sufflcient water. The Mill was also very difficult for motor vehicles to reach, which was also prob-ably a reason for its slow failure.

Ovingham. Tailor James Cook was the last of three generations, working until the day he died aged 84 in 1959. The shop then became, and remains, a grocers. Up to six tailors were employed on the first floor, reached by ladder, with the tailors sitting cross legged on low board seating. Mr Cook used to make the liveries for Lord Allendale's staff, and pitmen would come for block pattern suits - waiting outside on Saturdays to try them on. There is now a planning permission to replace the recent plate glass window with a shop front much more in keeping with the original building, in what is the heart of the village Conservation Area.

Branch End. Interior of the Longstaffe general store with Mr E (Ned) Longstaffe. The pre 1914 bakery was begun by Mrs Longstaffe who at first carried the bread around the area in a basket. Mr Longstaffe was a noted photographer of the area and published stereoscopic photographs in late Victorian/early Edwardian times. See page 37 for two such views of Mickley Square.

Ovington c. 1922. Looking east towards the British Legion Club built in wood by ex-servicemen after World War I. A forerunner of the existing CIU Club which has been totally rebuilt, and added to, in 1953 and 1971. The village is now well kept but this photo shows a dirt road and evidence of passing cows. The lady with the pails is carrying water. There were three communal taps - on the gable of Laburnum House, outside Evewood (the post office 1950-1973), and the one to which this lady is proceeding. The former post office is the third house from the right. Between it and The Ship Inn - also now known as Domingo's - is an alley to "The Maltings" which was used for a time for dances. The village is now without a public village hall.

HOMEWARD BOUND. OVINGTON

Ovington c1913. The east end of the village, at the blind bend in the road to Ovingham, just before it drops into what in the south of England would be called a hollow way. The view is the same in 1993, but none of the village farms are now dairy farms. Ovington Cottage with its lodge is on the left in the trees. Ovington House can be seen above the cottage gable on the right.

Ovington Brewery c.1920. Then owned by Robertson Lumley & Co latterly by the Emmerson Family, who still live in Ovington. Brewing ceased in Ovington in 1940 but a licence was held by the shop which Mr Emmerson operated until 1972. This brewery had a chain of ten public houses in the Tyne Valley, including The Bridge End Inn, Ovingham, three in Acomb and The Black Bull, Corbridge.

Ovington. The new saddlers shop opened in 1922 and, modified, still exists, but only as a shed. Mr Matt Huddlestone's former shop had been on the opposite side of the road, just to the east of The Highlander.

Ovington Sword Dancers 1932, at a competition held at Bywell Hall. Foster Oram, the instructor, is playing the tin whistle. From left to right the team was J Smith and Roland Cauldfield, Ted Smith and Jackie Mavin, Wm Armstrong and Jock Unwin. For a complete record the dancers performed Kirkby Malzeard to the tune of *Bobbie Shaftoe,* and Skelton, to *The Girl I left Behind Me.* The folk dance tradition continues today with The Ovingham Country Dance Club.

Ovington Prize Brass Band. Founded in 1862 and still in existence but no longer Ovington based. Here shown - not in uniform - just after World War II marching through Ovingham, between Grey Cottage and the post office. The band is thought to be proceeding to the Church Field Day, held on August Bank Holiday Monday - then at the beginning of the month.

BYWELL CASTLE

In Stocksfield Parish c.1925 the remains of the Bywell Dam. An old print shows this dam in 1756. It had been used by many water mills, but in July 1862 was partly dismantled. There is a current theory backed by archaeological evidence that Bywell was on a direct Roman Road between Ebchester and Halton Roman Fort, to the east of Portgate. At Bywell there were the remains of a Roman Bridge between the dam and the existing Bywell Bridge, which was started in August 1836. There is a further archaeological theory that this dam was commenced in Roman times, to allow the transport of goods by barge to the Corbridge Supply Base, and beyond, from the Roman port of South Shields.

Stocksfield Station (from the Round Hill) c.1930. Railway Cottages on the left were removed when the rail line was straightened to allow two trains to pass under the bridge, and a new road bridge was provided in 1968/69. The postcard shows various rail spurs and buildings which have been removed including the signal box, goods warehouse, and the coal yard. But the station master's cottage, the building now used by a slating and tiling firm, and the large Temperance Hotel (now Temperance House and Temperance Cottage) remain.

The current post office, which was transferred from the other side of the railway in 1960 is the second gable end building on the main roadside. The first gable end was of a shop, now a warehouse, and the adjacent yard was where pony and traps could be hired in the late 19th and early 20th century, for businessmen returning to Painshawfield Estate from the Newcastle trains.

Aero View, Stocksfield. 4779

This "Aero View" of Stocksfield c.1916/20 was taken in fact from the ground at Mount Pleasant, in the heavily mined area of Whinny Bank, looking west. From left to right are:- the upper length of Cade Hill Road - from Birches Nook, to the corner; the Baptist Chapel of 1905; Branch End Terrace; Birches Nook; Longstaffes Shop; Alexandra Terrace; part of Meadowfield Terrace; part of Brettonby Avenue, and on the far right in the distance is Stocksfield Station.

PAINSHAWFIELD, STOCKSFIELD.

Painshawfield Estate c. 1910, looking westerly down Painshawfield Road and then along the highest part of Cade Hill Road, to the corner. Snowdrop Cottage was the second house built on the then new estate, on the brow of the hill on the right, down Painshawfield Road. At the junction with New Ridley Road, on the left is the first Gazanni house. Harforth Lodge is to the right of Snowdrop Cottage. The Baptist Chapel built 1903 is centre right.

The Painshawfield Estate was founded in 1895-98. This 1916 view looking south east up Meadowfield Road towards New Ridley Road cannot be obtained today because of the growth of garden trees. Painshawfield is in the foreground running east to west. The land to the right is common, held by three Trustee/Owners to be maintained as Public Open Space. Three of the houses shown here were White House, - now called Ratchwood; Strathyre, - now Norland, and Cademuir -called Sunniside for a time but in 1993 back to Cademuir. Note the absence of houses on New Ridley Road. The estate appears largely as farmland, but had already been laid out for development. Original roads were Painshawfield Road, Well Road and Batt House Road, - all others were new.

Ridley Mill c.1930 with its metal overshot wheel in the valley of the Guess Burn. The Millpond is to the left at a higher level and can still be seen although empty. The Mill ceased to be supplied with water when the dam broke in 1942. There are still remnants of the wheel and mill today.

Branch End c.1910. Edward Longstaffe's Shop. He purveyed groceries, confectionery, bakery goods, cycles, fancy goods and he was also a professional photographer. Where was everything displayed or stored? - probably in the sheds (now the bakery), across the back lane. This photo shows the shop before it was extended to take in the adjacent house. Remodelling resulted in an extended symmetrical shop front with balcony over.

Branch End. 1914-18 War Celebrations, seen from the balcony of Longstaffe's extended and remodelled shop, looking up New Ridley Road (formerly known as The Minsteracres Turnpike, hence the Toll House on the right.) The West Wylam and Prudhoe Co-op can just be glimpsed on the left. It has had many reincarnations - publisher's office, bookshop, golfing shop and kitchen showroom, but it has been a Friends Meeting House for some time. Mickley Prize Silver Band is in the foreground.

Branch End 1921. Longstaffe's shop was the terminus for the Newcastle Corporation Blue Bus Service - which ran from August 1920 until 9 January 1938, initially connecting with the trams at Scotswood Bridge. This bus, BB2313, had a Straker-Squire chassis and engine, with a 35 seat body built by the Corporation at Byker Depot. Note the solid tyres and the protruding steering column. Andrew Liddle, founder of Liddles Garage at Branch End, was the driver. This bus was sold in July 1926 to a Mr Fleming of Neston in The Wirral Peninsula, and lasted until December 1940 - hopefully with pneumatic tyres. Its life was extraordinarily long for a bus of the early 1920s.

This rare Vulcan charabanc X9792, known as "The Betty", owned by Mr J Tulip of Harlow Hill, was always hired by Ovingham groups for trips. (Ovington people supported their local bus and lorry firm, operated by Mr T Armstrong, who ran "The Little Dene", and "The Ovingtonian".) This photo is particularly interesting as it shows the chara, with Mackintosh NAP tyres on the front wheels, while retaining the original hard tyres on the back - a very short-lived experiment just before balloon tyres became universal. The photo was probably taken in 1922/23. (Reproduced by kind permission of the Chris Warn Collection deposited at Northumberland County Record Office).

MICKLEY. 1667

Mickley. Main Road looking east c.1920 showing the United Methodist Free Church (the Gurney Chapel), which was demolished in the 1960s and replaced by four houses in the late 1980s. Next is a general dealers shop (part obscured by a wind blown bush) thought to be Nichols, but perhaps Stobarts, which was latterly a ladies hairdressers; and then as now, an electrical contractors office. The posed car was probably Mr Nichols' and one of the first in the area. A horse-drawn covered cart is delivering to the West Wylam and Prudhoe Co-op (which is now the Jiggery Pokery with the adjacent Bewick Printing Workshop complex) on the other side of the road. Beyond the Station Road Junction is High Row South which was backed by High Row North.

Mickley Square c.1914. It has been impossible to find any panoramic views of Mickley Square. These two posed shots are of individual houses. The photo on the right is particularly interesting as it is one of a joined pair sold by Mr Edward Longstaffe, who had an early photographic business - among others -at Branch End. Viewing the two together through a stereograph gave a 3D effect. It shows the Mickley Cycling Club. Who the mother and son are, at the door of their house, is unrecorded.

STATION ROAD, MICKLEY. 1666

Mickley Station Road, c.1920. Station Road led from the main Prudhoe - Hexham road downhill to a rudimentary station (called at very infrequently eg as little as once every Saturday to Newcastle, with a late train on alternate Saturdays), the ferry for Ovington, and the Hare and Hounds public house. The window on the extreme left is part of the Miners Arms. On the right is the large Blaydon Co-op with the Drapery Department protruding. The house with the gable beyond the tree is the end house in Long Row North, which was back to back with Long Row South. The entrance to Riding Dene is just beyond these rows.

Old Eltringham - a hamlet which used to be near Eltringham Farm House. This postcard of an old photograph (the original could date from the 1880s) shows cottages from the early to mid 1700s. The cattle trough, the far end white thatched cottage, slate roofed cottage with small windows and part of the next white cottage with thatched roof still existed in 1993 although the buildings had long been converted to animal sheds. As this is on private land, permission to view would be required.

Mickley Junction probably about 1930 was a hamlet at the foot of Station Bank - across the level crossing - of Railway owned houses with the Hare and Hounds pub on the Eltringham Farm side of the Newcastle and Carlisle railway. The Eltringham Ferry to the Ovington side of the river was about 75 yards to the left, which is probably where the girl with the dog was going. Behind the little boy on the extreme left are salmon nets hanging up to dry. Mickley Station/Halt was to the right of all the houses, but only a very rudimentary service was provided - from before 1884 to June 1915.

Ferry Boat and Salmon Boat. The operation of the Mickley Ferry was a condition on the tenant of the Hare and Hounds, Bernard Breweries-owned pub at Mickley Junction which continued until 1962/3. The main photo shows the last but one tenant - the Savage family, plus boy and dog as passengers. The boat, known by the family as The Waltzer was bought at South Shields for £3 per foot. It was a big boat and could carry up to 16 persons - at 2d for adults, 1d for children. The chalets on the Ovington bank were sometimes known as "African Village", the photo also shows The Quay Wall, on the Mickley side. The ferry was used by Ovington miners up to the 1930s going to and from the pits on the south side of the river. Its heydays were probably in the early 1940s when it was used by many Tyneside evacuees living in the chalets, and in the 1950s by holiday makers to "Boydies Beach" - now washed away. Salmon fishing, both by boat and rod, took place on the Tyne. The inset photo c.1930 shows a shallow draft (9") salmon boat at the Ovingham (commercial) Fishery in 1910. It is not being used for fishing, but for pleasure.

Eltringham Village, colliery and brickworks/pipeworks between 1910 and 1920. Access to this village was extremely difficult until Spring 1993, when the Prudhoe Bypass was opened. It was approached by very steep hairpin bends which necessitated Hammerite Paintworks Lorries reversing across the main A695 before descending the hairpins to the works. The view is from the south east looking across the colliery and pipeworks to the South, Middle and North Rows of the village, then across the valley to Ovington. The village was very self-contained with shop, chapel, reading room, playing field and quoits pitch. The school was situated up the hillside on what was the A695. Middle and South Rows were demolished about 1951- they had been constructed with a wooden exterior rubble infilling and then plastered over. Only ten houses now remain in North Row.

Eltringham pipeworks and colliery from the west probably before 1900. This view has been taken from a cracked glass plate. This colliery never recovered from the 1926 Miners Strike. Production from both the pipeworks and the brickworks was also affected, the brickworks closing first, and then the pipeworks in about 1975. The pipeworks was originally supplied by a narrow-gauge rope hauled railway with runs of six tubs carrying coal and clay from West Mickley Colliery. They made a terrible noise as they ran down to the pipeworks, using a short tunnel under the A69 to the rear of the Tyne Valley Garden Centre. The products from Eltringham were originally taken away by standard gauge NER/LNER trucks down to the sidings on The Quay, by another rope hauled system. The double track was very steeply curved and operated on a full truck down helping to pull a full truck up. The winding engine failed and the line was converted to narrow gauge, and the products transhipped into NER goods wagons on the Quay. After closure of the colliery the stables became the basis of a small farm. The Prudhoe Bypass cuts between the existing large building in the centre of the photograph and the ex-stables. The area of the pipeworks on the left, and the large building are now the Hammerite Paint Works.

Low Prudhoe from Ovingham Toll Bridge - before 1902 as the Adam and Eve pub is not obscured by the two storey Blaydon Co-op. The Colliery Rows on the right were School Row, and Castle Row West, and on the left Tyne Row, Chapel Row, and North Row backed by South Row. Tyne Row and the Methodist Chapel behind were the last to be cleared. The acetylene house for the three lamps on the toll bridge can be seen this side of the Station Masters red brick house.

Low Prudhoe, looking across Prudhoe Station between 1896 and 1902. The Adam and Eve pub is on the right and Tyne Row on the opposite side of the road. Prudhoe Station was then much more extensive. The single storey red brick station had been removed and replaced by two perspex shelters by 1980. The mystery of why Prudhoe did not have an attractive stone built station of the 1830s, similar to Wylam, Stocksfield, Riding Mill and Corbridge has been solved by Dr Fawcet. In the early days of railways, stations were built according to who the railway's directors thought would use their stations. Evidently there were not sufficient gentry in the locality of Prudhoe Station for a stone station, so a wooden shed was provided. Discussions with agents for the landowner in 1846/7 for the site of a better station were fruitless. A platform and stone shed were built for passengers in 1852. Finally, after the line became part of the NER, a standard red brick station was supplied in 1884 - and probably opened in 1885. This lasted until 1971.Prudhoe area population began to expand in the late 1870s as more pits and drifts developed, which resulted in more rail sidings and goods facilities at Prudhoe. Prudhoe colliery was just to the left of the path which led from Masters Close Farm and Mickley. It was a pit without a heap as waste was restacked underground. There were ten more pits and drifts immediately to the west round Eltringham and the pipeworks. The vast output was transported from Prudhoe Station sidings and the Quay Wall sidings.

Prudhoe Station. The name "Prudhoe for Ovingham" Station was only used from 3 May 1937 until March 1971. When this photo was taken, c.1910, it was Prudhoe, and has reverted again to Prudhoe. This shows an engine at the North British Railway Company which negotiated rights to use North Eastern Railway Company tracks in 1863 between Hexham and Newcastle - but only to the extent of three passenger and two goods trains per day. The passenger service operated between Hawick - Riccerton Junction - Kielder - Bellingham - Hexham - Prudhoe and Newcastle. Such a service lasted until October 1956.

Stocksfield Station from the east between 1910/20. The station was built c.1838. A rather nice signal gantry is prominent, controlling access to the down up lines and giving access to a holiday loop, almost to what is now the Cricket Field. Note the gas lamps, including the very unusual position of the lamp on the footbridge above the tracks. Perhaps the ladder and taper are for the staff to light the lamps. This photo shows the old bullhead rail. Beyond the footbridge is the old roadbridge which takes the A695 over the track with a very much widened new bridge, built about twenty years ago. The building on the left - a warehouse - was removed about 15 years ago. A signalbox is on the platform for Newcastle.

Thomas Bewick's birthplace, Cherryburn, Eltringham. Thought to be from an original photograph about 1860 and showing it in use as agricultural buildings. The Bewick Trust converted it to its internal arrangements in Thomas Bewick's time from plans drawn by his son and only found in 1987. Now National Trust property, it is hoped it will be restored to a heather thatch roof. The door on the right has been removed - and a window has been inserted in what was the kitchen; the door on the left is the entrance to the dairy beyond; and to the left a "new" window had to be inserted to light what was, in Bewick's time, the small parlour.